# The Fire Garden

Paul Wilson

To Kelly

may 6, 1988

# The Fire Garden

Paul Wilson

COTEAU BOOKS

Some of these poems have been broadcast on CBC Radio on "Ambience." and some have been published in Briarpatch, CVII, event, Grain, NeWest Review, Northern Light, Three-Legged Coyote, Whetstone, and in the Coteau Books anthology Heading Out: The New Saskatchewan Poets. An earlier version of "Home Lives" was also broadcast on CBC Radio's "Ambience."

Cover art by Esther Warkov
Burning Rubble on the Prairie #1. 1984 (pencil on paper)
Collection of the artist
Cover and book design by Carolyn Deby
Produced in co-operation with Publication Associates Ltd.
Printed by Hignell Printing Ltd.
The text is set in 11 pt. Novarese Medium

The author would like to thank the following: fellow members of The Correction Line, who were the first to read and comment on these poems: Edna Alford, Lorna Crozier, Joe Rosenblatt, and Geoff Ursell, for their comments and suggestions: the Saskatchewan School of the Arts and Saskatchewan Writers/Artists Colonies, where many of the poems were written; and the Saskatchewan Writers Guild. Special thanks to my family. Elizabeth George, Anne Szumigalski, and Nik Burton, who have all (in their own way) encouraged my writing.

The publisher gratefully acknowledges the assistance of the Saskatchewan Arts Board and the Canada Council in the publication of this book.

**Saskatchewan Arts Board**

Canadian Cataloguing in Publication Data

Wilson. Paul, 1954-
    The fire garden

    (The Wood Mountain series : 5)
    Poems.
    ISBN 0-919926-64-9 (bound) — ISBN 0-919926-63-0 (pbk.)

    I. Title. II. Series.

PS8595.I47F5 1987    C811'.54    C87-098048-3
PR9199.3.W44F5 1987

## coteau books

Thunder Creek Publishing Co-operative
Distribution office                 Editorial/Promotion office
Box 239. Sub # 1                    2337 McIntyre Street
Moose Jaw. Saskatchewan             Regina. Saskatchewan
S6H 5V0                             S4P 2S3

For My Mother & Father

# Heart Line

This Skill . . . . . . . . . . . . . . . . . . . . . . . . . . . . . . . . . . . . . . . . 2
The Truss . . . . . . . . . . . . . . . . . . . . . . . . . . . . . . . . . . . . . . . . . 3
Spoils . . . . . . . . . . . . . . . . . . . . . . . . . . . . . . . . . . . . . . . . . . . . 4
Snow House . . . . . . . . . . . . . . . . . . . . . . . . . . . . . . . . . . . . . . . 5
The White Beach . . . . . . . . . . . . . . . . . . . . . . . . . . . . . . . . . . . 6
Diving . . . . . . . . . . . . . . . . . . . . . . . . . . . . . . . . . . . . . . . . . . . 7
Rites For Holding The Day
    Spotted  Slough . . . . . . . . . . . . . . . . . . . . . . . . . . . . . . . 8
    Dog . . . . . . . . . . . . . . . . . . . . . . . . . . . . . . . . . . . . . . . . . 9
    Instrument . . . . . . . . . . . . . . . . . . . . . . . . . . . . . . . . . . 10
    Furnace . . . . . . . . . . . . . . . . . . . . . . . . . . . . . . . . . . . . 11
    Mirror . . . . . . . . . . . . . . . . . . . . . . . . . . . . . . . . . . . . . 12
Holding  Out . . . . . . . . . . . . . . . . . . . . . . . . . . . . . . . . . . . . 13
Buffalofish . . . . . . . . . . . . . . . . . . . . . . . . . . . . . . . . . . . . . . 14
Ice . . . . . . . . . . . . . . . . . . . . . . . . . . . . . . . . . . . . . . . . . . . . 15
Buffalo Lake. Buffalo Stone . . . . . . . . . . . . . . . . . . . . . . . 16

# Frieda Buffalocalf . . . . . . . . . . . . . . . . . . . . . . . . 17

# Home Lives . . . . . . . . . . . . . . . . . . . . . . . . . . . . . . . . 29

# *Living Pictures*

Snap Shot . . . . . . . . . . . . . . . . . . . . . . . . . . . . . . . . . . . . 50
Dreaming: The Third Marine . . . . . . . . . . . . . . . . . 51
Living Picture/1882 . . . . . . . . . . . . . . . . . . . . . . . . . 52
Living Picture/March 18, 1982
El Salvador . . . . . . . . . . . . . . . . . . . . . . . . . . . . . . . . . 53
Leaning Man . . . . . . . . . . . . . . . . . . . . . . . . . . . . . . . . 54
prints . . . . . . . . . . . . . . . . . . . . . . . . . . . . . . . . . . . . . . 55
Rival . . . . . . . . . . . . . . . . . . . . . . . . . . . . . . . . . . . . . . . 56
Shooting Script . . . . . . . . . . . . . . . . . . . . . . . . . . . . 57
*Channel Forty:*
*Your Salvation Station* . . . . . . . . . . . . . . . . . . . . . . . 58
Bluebeard's Widow and
The Commerce of Mirrors . . . . . . . . . . . . . . . . . . . . 61
Popcorn In Victoria Park . . . . . . . . . . . . . . . . . . . . 62
Last of The Las Vegas Icons . . . . . . . . . . . . . . . . . 63
Carnival Stones . . . . . . . . . . . . . . . . . . . . . . . . . . . . . 65
Waiting Room . . . . . . . . . . . . . . . . . . . . . . . . . . . . . . . 66
The Man is Faceless . . . . . . . . . . . . . . . . . . . . . . . . . 67
This Time See . . . . . . . . . . . . . . . . . . . . . . . . . . . . . . . 68
In Every Fire a Garden . . . . . . . . . . . . . . . . . . . . . . 71
prayer in the event
of a fast blue winter . . . . . . . . . . . . . . . . . . . . . . . . 72

# Heart Line

## This Skill

Mother, this skill can be traced
to my fourth summer. The act
of recalling pain. Always so little
to begin with

our feet pad cool
clay, you hold my hand
and you are crying. My head is hot,
I don't want to slip from your hand,
or smell lilac, I want to hold my breath
until ears fill with blood, do something to explain
how the ardour passes from you
to me, you crying and I holding back.
But there is sleep
in my legs and you lift me. Your hands
burn where they touch my skin.
I raise an arm to shade my eyes
and the sun turns over: a flat stone
in the cup of my palm.

## The Truss

Tonight, doing chores
you fell,
wrenched something inside,
the pain, a pitch-fork
through your gut when you tried to stand,
when you stood and broke straw bales
for the calves.

I help you with the truss,
a tangled confusion in your hands.
I draw the elastic belt around your waist,
slowly putting pressure on the hernia.
You bite your lip,
wait before speaking:

> Pain is syrup to an old soldier.
> Took a lot worse, '42 at Casino
> shrapnel ripped up my arm to the elbow,
> was three hours before a corpsman saw it.
> Me cracking questions about my funnybone,
> will I ever laugh again Doc?

Father, am I to carry these words
to a death, return again to the silence
that ends stories of war?
The silence that comes over you now,
the heel of your hand moving
to stroke the pain deeper.

## Spoils

Neighbourhood wars were fought
with crabapples, unripe.
We would climb up through trees and strip
the heavy green branches with rakes,
crush the apples under our feet,
pocket the spoils.

And late in summer
we'd bite edges into weapons,
slice apples in half with our teeth;
chewing one half, launching the other.
When apples ripened, the pace
of war slowed. Our mouths full,
we'd stand in range,
taunting the enemy,
licking the acid
from our hands.

## Snow House

I kept pen-pals in Trinidad,
Brazil, Panama (my sister had a love
of exotic stamps), I listened to voices.
These children wrote one page
letters on thin blue paper,
told me of where they lived, white rooms,
tropical plants in arched windows,
the constant perfume of gardens.

I wrote of snow
drifted to the eaves.
They misunderstood,
thought that my house
my home was made of snow.
I let them keep belief
in the permanence of winter.
I wrote lies
of a snow house and of my need
to punch holes in white
and flowerless walls.

## The White Beach

Lindy: his stories
work an undoing,
the way he stands
arms flapping, voice running on
about the war, he can still rattle off
death tolls: Normandy, Dieppe, Dunkirk.

I want to redream
the maples that used to stand
in the median on Main Street.
It's paved now, but stand
just where they were,
look due east,
and you can see the beach,
the water where I nearly drowned
when I was nine.
Lindy swore he was the one
who saved me.

And I wish those trees were back
so I could climb into the high branches
for a better view of the white beach;
gulls scattered on the shore,
and the boy wading
out past the point.

**Diving**

                              They found you
floating, feet swollen in your boots, arms bound
by a jean jacket, pulled over your head
and gathered at your neck.

I think of the kid you were, the cool you had.
Nights I slept over, you talking in circles, breasts
your hands explored. Softly breathing
names, rolling them out like felt pennants
pinned above your bed. Weekends I followed you to the reservoir,
watched you dive from the raft; swimming easy strokes,
arms arcing water as you circled me. You pulled me in once,
hooted, "Swim, swim now!" I floundered in my jeans and sneakers,
before you caught an arm and saved me. I stayed on the bank
after that, wading in up to the waist.

I can see you drinking, throwing empty beer bottles in a high arc
aimed at the raft. But I cannot see you diving dead drunk,
knowing the depth, remembering how you counted strokes from shore
to the raft, how you swam down to bring up fistfuls of mud.

The raft exists for the boy, his tanned legs kicking at air
as he plunges into green water. I stop my breath, the white soles
of his feet flash like fins and vanish.

# RITES FOR HOLDING THE DAY

### 1

## Spotted Slough

It could never be a "lake",
the name it carries on the map
in the village office.

Named by someone
who had never seen it.
*Spotted* L.
centred in a blue oval,
the blue
map-makers use
for all bodies of water,
alive or dead.

He knows the water
is green with life,
it's not dead.
But he ties the word to
the smell of seasons
moving under water,
cat-tails leaning into death,
the stench, decay
beneath the algae.
He could leave
if it had not been days
since the hunt,
if the scent
had left his hands.

He could give it a name
of his own,
if they hadn't put the lie
in his head.

**2**

## Dog

He dreams a dog sings,
loose in the house licking sugar from the bowl
on the kitchen table, clawing linen and pillows
in his mother's bedroom. I *spied a young cowboy*,
the dog stinks of whisky, staggers on four black legs,
singing *all dressed in white linen*
the dog stretches out on the bed
straight as a man, his voice
breaks the dream *as cold as the clay*, this song,
this song his father knew.

**3**

**Instrument**

Once he played for a black
bird, dead in an empty box car.
He danced the blues, the bird wild
inside his head, he pushing air,
sucking in
the rattle of wings;
spit and dust
in the reeds.

There are ways
of blocking discord
at the end of the tongue,
ways of listening,
close melodies
his father never learned.

Days he will hold
the instrument
mute in a closed hand.

**4**

**Furnace**

The furnace is burning.
He can hear it in the dark, a constant
exhalation, a sun, frozen
in eclipse. He stands in a rectangle
of light below the trapdoor
and waits.

He waits for the furnace to burn out,
for ice to cut through walls
and lie in the furnace bed. He waits
for his father to emerge, a fine dust
on his peak-cap, in the furrows
between his eyebrows, stooping to spit
black.

He waits for the sun
to burn cold.

**5**

**Mirror**

He folds the mirror,
its wings settle
against his temples
and he slips through the interior
of an imperfect prism.

There are points where he ceases
to be visible, where his life
recedes into nothingness,
but he returns to images of himself.
In angles of incidence and reflection
he glimpses men, fragments of twin brothers,
a symmetry of faces in groups of six,
like pall bearers, by-
standers.

In the planes of glass
they turn away
and he recognizes, in his profile,
the face of his own father.

## Holding Out

Friends, will you write of your son's progress? You remember my last visit, long nights between equinox and Christmas. I drank schnapps in your kitchen, Inge you drew the serum into a syringe small enough to be a toy in a child's game. What was it the doctors said: *he has experienced a flutter, a faltering* — a sort of amnesia of the heart? Barry, after the injection he howled and you walked with him. But do you remember the song I made up on the spot and when you held him out to me he fell silent to my strange whistling? It was as if he had forgotten his small vocabulary of pain. While he slept you talked of giving up the farm before the banks closed in. You would find work in an overseas oil field. You talked of returning to the land when it could be done on your own terms. What has happened my friends?

You must write of your new home, of things no longer foreign to you.

## Buffalofish

Runoff hammers through
                    culverts,
slicing at the bank. I wade
                    further down stream,

casting into shadows on the creek bottom.
                    Jackfish
brush my spoon, I reel in weeds.

                              On the bank
a buffalofish hoisted in air,
poplar spear run through slack gills,
                              planted

in mud. (The fish has not evolved,

this is how we've always dealt with suckers.)

I move down, dead fish smell
        a liquid pain
at the back of my mouth. Current
stings my calves, I want to fall
face down in shallows, easing into darkwater.

But this creek, cold vein in the land, circles me.
I can't leave the buffalofish:
blunt sundial:
silver ellipse of mouth

        traversing
the southern sky.

## Ice

there are spoon-shaped
smudges beneath my eyes,
my beard smells of potatoes
days when there is sun
I eat late
tired of fish dreams,
butter in their bellies

carrots slowly turn wooden
in my pockets,
loaf shrinks, a hard nut
behind my ear
how many hopeless nights
before ice breaks
and lake feeds

how many nights will I dream of a boat
to hold the days in

## Buffalo Lake, Buffalo Stone
(for Ken)


I imagine the lake
beyond the town,
blue in the sun. We were told
that from the air you could see
a sleeping buffalo
in the body of water.

On a slender
island called *The Eye*
I found a skull,
holding it to my face I lowered horns
and charged the stunted trees.
It was easy to dream
a great herd in the shallow bay,
see the shoreline vanishing around me.

I carry that image with me
an effigy:
my head stuck in a buffalo skull,
my dream caught in the ribs of this lake.

\*


I learned later the Blackfoot
chose to see buffalo
in fossils they found in river beds.
They marked each stone with a heart line:
a line from mouth to heart,
heart to mouth.
A line to let
the spirit speak.

# Frieda Buffalocalf

when I asked you
Frieda, where is home    you showed me
a world from the eyes of a magpie    your hands
shaping spirits from shadow:
a badger running on a fallow field
deer standing in slow August rain
an arrow-head of geese
on the face of the moon

one night you slept in the weeds
under the fire-escape, hands clamped
between your thighs for warmth

I found you in the morning
a grasshopper on your forehead
interpreting the dream behind your eye-lids

Frieda you could've owned
that juke box; the quarters
you plugged into it
pushing buttons for songs
you couldn't hear
      the voice
of your John drowning
out the words

vibrations on the drum
of your ear, hands under
the table, moving on your lap
and you rocking
in three-quarter time

last summer
your brothers found you
alone in the bar     drunk
they brought news, a death
was it your mother
          your father
they wanted to take you home
but you bit the ear of one
spat blood in the other's face
as they carried you out

first thing next morning,
you showed up at the bar
a case of empties
rattling under each arm

he stumbled to your table
slid a hand along your shoulder,
caressed your neck
with his fingers,
then cupped your breast, beer
in the other hand

not once while he drank
did he look at you
not even when he motioned
follow, as if he
would lead you through
bush, but he didn't see
your face, he didn't hear
your laughter, you leaning back
his ears filling with the muted hiss
of a dying lake bird
a hiss in the throat,
his heel on the neck

it was the night of the first snow
that stayed     Frieda, it fell outside
your window, did you watch and want
to turn wet flakes on your tongue
did he watch you at the window, his words
a broken bottle against your silence

show me bones, Frieda, the powder
of bones pressed
into your palms

I find you upright
in an armchair, blood
on the bed, sheets twisted
to a red floor

the key still in the door,
and nothing registers
but a finger-painting
my kid brought home once
remembered the name he gave: sun coming
up sun going down
all mixed together

we close the bar at midnight
everyone is out by 12:30
the tables are cleared glasses washed
                the cop said a hunting knife was used
                there were multiple wounds
the night clerk has instructions not to rent the room
                I lock the key
                behind the till
when everyone is gone I sit and sip a double scotch
                and listen to the silence
                in the bar, your silence
                moving from table to table

who will keep the magpies out, Frieda
they have come through winter
to perch on your collarbones

I cannot keep them out
they stow your eyes under wings,
scavenging the cruel
spring

your brothers borrow a pick-up
and purple gas to bring you back
from the city, borrow
rope and tarpaulin
to tie down the corners
of your coffin, borrow
a radio, propped on the dash
for the long ride home,
turned up full, mostly static
and wind through the tarp
pulling at the ropes,
pulling at their voices,
drumming crazy songs and the highway
rolling black over white hills

each night they set
fire to your plot
and still they cannot
break earth

they watch the fire
as if it were garden
but after two weeks
of cold from the arctic
they are losing patience
and talk of putting you
to fire
letting your ashes seep
through frost with spring

sometimes they believe
the cold is your doing
and the fire your last wish
but each night they rake
the wood coals, they rake
the coals dead

# Home Lives

☐

there are days
when she can no longer
move her life
she sits
in the rocker and stares
into the street     balked
by a dull smouldering
in the heart of things

slowly rocking
herself back into the world
of hard light
dreaming the house
and flames     seeing the house
go up in flames

☐

sun thru cut glass
shoots spikes of violet light
along walls    she moves
to the door
sees the ghost
child on the front step and turns
to pleasure her body can't
contain    she feels warmth
on her hand as she
reaches for the brass
door knob

□

she would have a boarder
new pastels
in the back room
   quiet disappearances
   routine arrivals
a voice
to answer her call
to supper

he arrives with boxes
of books and dark panel-board
for the walls
of his room
his study

□

she is a sleepwalker      fat
with dreaming      her face
tight in expectation
stumbling from room to room
         with a sense that eggs
are to be gathered      in bed
she felt their fragile gestures
at her thighs
she walks into corners but eggs
lie hidden
cloistered in warmth her dream
cannot move

she finds china eggs
on saucers in the oak cabinet
she holds one      its coolness
on her forehead
on her lidded eyes
a static vowel
her open mouth

□

the boarder finds a drawing
in the bottom of a dresser     face down
        it is the drawing of a young child
there is a resemblance:     her eyes
        but the lines reveal
a hurried artist
        it could be anyone's child
he studies the drawing
looking at the spaces where her likeness
        surfaces
and is lost

□

it is always the ghost child
his blue toque at the window
his nose flat
against the cold glass

she squats
her reflection is a thin shadow

her darkness eclipses
his pale face

□

he is impatient for the first snow
storm    he listens from his room
to her movements    he knows the house
will not struggle    he hums to music
on his clock radio    his voice
drifts thru her morning

he imagines her bending
to put on a stocking    his thin song
piling up at the foot
of her bed

□

a plate breaks
clean up the middle     she pulls
two half moons from the soapy water
her thumb bleeds where an edge
has cut her


drying his hands
he finds the blood
stain     hidden
in the folds
of a white towel

□

the ghost child will not answer
to his given name
          he won't come inside
on the coldest days
          she stands on the deck
looking over the fence
          to the snow fields beyond

fields where children play fox
and geese     dig tunnels
in the drifted snow     she will not
call him again
          there is a room inside
that is empty
     she has filled it
with the sound of his name

◻

he brings her a gift of three
crystal pyramids
                she strings them
at different lengths in the east window
in their many faces a small
angular horizon tips
forward    she rubs finger prints
from the lightness of glass
notes the time sun shifts
below the roof line

□

the hot cast iron handle
has marked him
                        red welts
across four fingers

she blames herself
for leaving the pan
            on the stove
                    she reaches deep
into the jar for what is left
of the salve

he comes to her
with his hand closed
then opens it ever so carefully
as if he were holding the end
of a thin red cord

□

rough wood rolls slowly in the lathe
he applies the gouge     thin shavings fall away
he wets his lips     a cove
opens beneath his fingers

he turns
legs for tables
he will never build
stacked in the corner
each leg is shaped by
a singular desire

□

       to have the plant live
she would sing to each split
leaf     leaning as if to kiss the open
ended mouths    tonguing
water syllables — philodendron
she would press hymns
into the moist soil
she would sing awake
the green will
of the dying plant

□

she rubs her cheek bones
where skin prickles
as if cold had found scars

he wears a balaclava
making connections under the hood
positive  positive    negative
negative    signaling to her    start

she shivers    turns the key
eyes closed for one clean shock

□

the morning of a blizzard
she dreams the child swims
between the crabapple
and the back fence     stroking
into high drifts
his hair white with snow
his face turned away from her
his breath moving
above the frozen lawn
his feet kicking up dry snow

☐

        she dreams
the storm is over

she hears the sun
walk above, the sound
of light on snow
ghost sun always
one beat
behind

in her chest
blood raises

a reflex of laughter

□

she will not answer
but he knows where
she is     in the middle
of his day he sees her
in one room then another
unplugging extensions     breaking down
lines he holds

☐

spoon gathers
flecks of light

spoon to stir
their coffee     his sugar
her cream      the spoon


placed in the centre
within reach of the other
the silent lie

passed like a weapon

47

□

in gray twilight
        she pulls
a child's sleigh over fields
beyond the yard     breaking snow
the crust scrapes her legs     the sleigh
glides over the surface     runners straddling
her foot steps
              she looks back
the house is lost
streetlights stand up: thin flames
on a jagged line of roof-tops and fences

she leaves the sleigh
over-turned
at the bottom of
a stubble slope     and walks
in a new direction

# Living Pictures

## Snap Shot

a thin young man removes
a black t-shirt by an unmade bed
face thrust down     his arms reach back
fabric pinched in fingers
he pulls at his shoulder blades

but shift the image slightly
and a body quivers     his head
slumps in a sack
bound at the shoulders his arms
tied back     broken wings

I give this one a history
a presence
strips of light warm his face
his slack fingers curl
like fronds at the edge of the black hem
he has been dying for years

knowing this I could tear
the hunched body     peel back the hood

but he is mine to keep
he is an absence I'm trying to fill
a hostage in a country I can't return to
he is with me even when I turn away
this impression of him breathing
the smell of his skin

## Dreaming: The Third Marine

I am pouring coffee
for myself and the marine across
the table who's writing home
we have it black since another marine
is hunched in the refrigerator and will blow
the head off anyone who opens the door

a third marine
runs invisible line
thru paper wings
building a mobile
in my living room
he says *these are breasts*
*buttocks of my lovers*
*back home      polaroid cut outs*
*the women of this country turn*
*away from my camera*
*they don't understand the politics*
*of dance      soon they will learn*
*that this is a partnership*
the first marine crumples his letter
into a ball and begins again
the third marine strings bayonets
as if they were christmas ornaments
and hangs them in my kitchen window      says
*I will show them the sweet gestures*
*of freedom      and they will appear*
*as brides      bleeding happiness*
*in all my photographs*
*with head and hands held*
*still in the tropical light*

51

## Living Picture / 1882

the magician moves
in his sequence
unconnected to a world
outside the frame

he pulls the trick
behind two black fans
head in the box
no head on his shoulders
head on his shoulders
no head in the box
at centre stage the magician
reverses and repeats
the illusion inside
the picture for audience outside
the frame and for one man
in the second row who turns
frowning in disbelief
each time the trick is performed

## Living Picture/ March 18, 1982: El Salvador

the cameraman is hit
              picture
thrown to sun

scraping blue
                        the spine
of a red clay roof
                              empty window
focusing black        panning
to the soldier      who fires
who kills the picture

                        a second
time slow
motion
soldier     aims straight/fires
                              at the camera/drops
                              picture/camera/
                                     man

## Leaning Man

He leans toward the fall
of his own voice
angular in his throat
his need to forget
as he reads     editing
eternity on the supper
hour news


In his palms
pages
shrink
to syllables
his words appear
as bodies: he reads
the daily count:
Sabra    Shatila    Grenada    San Salvador
words that root tongue

**prints**

*you are free to wash*
ensure your hands are clean and dry
*shake blood into your fingers* stand in front of the table
*we will make you innocent* be careful
do not get ink on your clothes
*your left hand empty* make a fist with your right hand,
thumb protruding, use light pressure
*use right pressure* place your thumb                    '
*under a photograph*
*a strange face* being careful not to twist
*clean print* lift the inked thumb
*of your left* holding the form with your right
and using the same pressure, place the thumb
*your confession* in the space provided     again be careful
*on the dark page* do not twist your thumb

## Rival

It's come to sabotage
between us:
each morning I check the bread box
for bombs.

He steals my newspapers.
I find them days later
at the bottom of the stairs
coffee stains blossoming
among the pages.
He watches sports
tapes football over my opera.
He sleeps in my best chair.

He occupies the rooms
with no windows and once a week
throws open the doors
filling my life with his dead air.

## Shooting Script


                   this is big budget stuff
a fireball     human shadows
burned into a wall


a camera on rails shoots
the salt flats     they brief you:
this is ground zero
you are a standin/stuntman     now
cover your eyes     imagine
you are about to die
above your head
an aquamarine sky fades to white
and the script calls
for special effects final frames     nothing
like the way you
see it     a splice at
the point of impact

## Channel Forty: Your Salvation Station

I

Horizontal hold flips
as Nathan Winter comes on; leather voice
bracing words, hand raised, a raft in flood
lights: B*rothers, sisters, we are at the abyss!*

Tonight his voice is a rock slide.
It buries you in the belief
that stone flows on Blood Mountain.

II

At the river Nathan is folding ice,
hands shaping tidy bricks, stockpiles
for the construction of drowning pools.

He kisses each blue brick,
wetting lips on the clarity of miracle,
then passes them to his apprentice
who removes fingerprints from their faces
with his steamy breath. But see how he uses
a chisel and hammer when Nathan turns away.

III

Sunday morning Nathan
waits in the alley where an immaculate
garbage truck delivers, growling breakfast
onto his shoes.

He wades in, speaking
testimonial words,
places egg shells over eyes, rolls
bacon rinds between molars, wishes
flies a good-good morning, sprinkles
blessed coffee grounds, skips
for the Lord and jingles:
*Hallelujah, hallelu*
                    *jah!*

Filling the dead air
with his joy.

IV

In primetime Nathan
sells skin and a book:
*Four E-Z To Do Video Miracles*
*Yes brothers, sisters, you too can ease*
*pain, a vision of pain.*

He grins neon and the skin
settles in his arms like a ghost,
a figure floats toward you;
it is the price Nathan is prepared to kill for,


and you sit
there as open
as a child
before a fall.

## Bluebeard's Widow and
## The Commerce of Mirrors


he was a tabloid magnate     and his papers
covered murder as if it were a spectator sport

I survived him     (his high blood-pressure)     I kept him
transfixed by illusions: red-winged black birds

vanished into my open palms then reappeared
on my shoulders     the colour gone from their wings

soon he was filling his great halls with trick
mirrors and I was given a menagerie of props

but when voices of his dead wives spoke to me
from the margins of his front page photographs

I began to keep one room ahead of my husband
I took sanctuary in the commerce of mirrors

I was the black bear at his table     the lion
who slept till noon in the oval glass above his bed

and he would rage at my reverse image     no longer
his wife but some other     not always human

## Popcorn in Victoria Park

The man who hates crows doesn't know why
they live here. He's thought of calling the Mayor
on a radio talk show, but decided that the Mayor would know
nothing about crows. The man curses from his bench;
they startle him, descending from elms, black and cackling
they devour popcorn he sets out
for pigeons. He sees explosions
in air, feathers falling like ash from the sky.
He wishes the other people on the bench
would help him capture one, holding those wings
so he could strangle the bird.
He doesn't want a quiet execution,
let it be a shotgun celebration
and he would burn the carcasses
at noon, on any sidewalk.

Looking for wing-flash beyond foliage,
seeing a crow in every elm, the man who hates
crows holds a jumbo bag of popcorn
close to his chest.

## Last of The Las Vegas Icons

1

the billboard that blocks off the las vegas skyline is a cave a giant face peers out but all its features are dark we come to bow in the mid-day sun and whisper at the pale neon *frank frank frank come back to us* and we come here knowing it's a bad bet because ol' blue eyes says he'd rather golf for a grand a stroke at pebble beach but the high rollers are here with their midnight black lincolns and peach cadillacs and we spend an hour on bleachers provided by the los nova hotel and we watch for a sign a twitch an ethereal voice from the face a voice that will push back the darkness and draw us into the hazy brilliance of a nelson riddle orchestration but at dusk when the city flares we climb aboard the bus and the driver circles the billboard one more time with his lights on high beam we glimpse the eyes and they're like two great sequins faded to the pigment of the desert sky

.

2

we have to take the body
seriously     love it like a resurrection
but it's really a work of art
when you think     every detail
is edible     we fall silent
when he's rolled into the spotlight
wearing a blue sport coat
this is the king
in his ballad days
his natural stance
but slightly taller than in real life
          feet spread wide     left knee
          bent precisely where the beat
          moves him     his body leaning
          toward the mike
          the glaze on his lips
reflecting light into an oblonged halo
and overhead
          love me tender
          love me true
and we start as his big hits play
we file by quietly
one at a time with a cheese knife
and a ritz cracker
and we circle around again
until all that is left
are his white shoes
and they are made of ice

## Carnival Stones
Spain, 1984

Take three stones, senor,
stones for the caged
rabbit. They are only
a quarter, senor.

Take one in your hand,
fold fingers over jagged edges and aim
for the ebony of eye.
The rabbit is blind, it will not leap
until the stone strikes.

The stones, senor.

Carefully picked
from Malaga beaches
three will kill
if your aim is good.

A good cause; we buy
white carnations
for the cloak of the virgin
to carry through our village
on the Holy Week
of Brotherhood.

## Waiting Room

i

who's she waiting for
with her feet bare
and toe nails painted
blood colour
ten dainty moons
rising and falling
as she crosses and uncrosses
her legs

who's under the knife
as she chews her gum, turns
the pages of a magazine
who's waiting for her
in a drugged dream
do they see her, stirring the air
her white foot,
lifted
to the narrow heel
of the moon

ii

I read the headline
    PRESIDENT LIVES
    STOMACH TRANSPLANT A SUCCESS

    the photograph
is of the President sharing his bed
with a panda
    both are smiling
they are the only ones in the room
who are smiling

66

iii

the husband
is drunk again
he brings dead flowers
pot balanced     on his knee
chrysanthemums sway
under his influence
he lowers his head     breathes deep

the dark blossoms
kiss his face


iv

a woman down the hall
moans, pain lifted
from a wheelchair, she tries
to form words but can't
I want to hear her tell
how it hurts, words that trail
like a news flash,
like an assassination attempt

there is a need for my own movements
to be painful, my own breath
to be suspect, I want a quick
recovery

## The Man is Faceless
Japan, 1985


He is faceless as a peeled orange,
as a gutted pomegranate,
faceless as a mashed chocolate,
as a whispered threat
in a market place crowd

O *poison*, he says, I *have cyanide,*
*a seed of death with your lunch*

Let him come and show the pulp
of his face     let him pose with his syringe
and we will construct a face of handkerchiefs
bound in pigwire     we will fashion ears
as flags for his deadly games
we will cut and paste the face
of a suicide from the morning paper

and O yes we will give him a name
we will paint his name on subway walls
and when he has a name he will be harmless
as the old man who complains
of my oranges, sweet chocolate,
my bitter green apples

## This Time See

this time see
thru the tinted glass
into the back seat
of the black limousine future
where men in white tuxedos
write high concepts
we assume and are asked to forget

and we don't ask about tribes who build fires
along this freeway *they are only burning straw*
says the man behind the wheel
who speaks a language of reduction
but there is a deftness in his words
he talks with a mouth full of water
his tongue is drowning     his tongue
is high and dry

    or he says:
*a dead senator turns up as a barker*
*for the seven wonders sex show*
*but no one recognizes his face*
*or his forgiveness     and one night*
*he's stabbed by a sailor*
*who doesn't like his looks but grass sprouts*
*from the senator's wounds     and a crowd gathers*
*to watch his miraculous death*

or he says:
       *in a ghost crater in arizona*
       *an elaborate fire escape appears*
       *a steel staircase ascending     unsupported*
       *to a tar-paper door     and millions*
       *travel to this place     blessing each step*
       *but no one finds a way to leave*
       *backing down in file     though whole flights*
       *bow under their weight*

or he says:
*astronomers on satellite tv claim*
*they have found a hoop of light*
*a white fuse they name for themselves*
*excited bell boys they carry*
*photographs with white arrows that point*
*to an object     still in the dark*
*they hold up holograms     they hold the rim*
*of the universe in their gloved hands*

                        listen
                        to the man
behind the wheel     see
he talks
                  but his tongue
                    is still

## In Every Fire a Garden

tonight in the village

        dogs speak

a common urgency

        tethered

they run in

        out of my

                hearing

                tonight

san salvador      has fallen

down    they can't get

images to us    fast enough

        listen

in every fire a garden

is consumed    in every

house    death    and walls

    fold:      broken

    hands on breast

        bones

**prayer in the event
of a fast blue winter**


let the bag ladies rise up
in the sweet bed of their belongings

carrying fuel, corn
brooms, properties of fire

in the blue, blue storm
let them climb a spiral wind

throwing off overcoats, scarves
slowly forgetting their lives

ascending thru a cloud of ice
their lungs chalked by winter

let them set fire to their tongues
breathing amber flames against the blizzard

let their hands meet in the air
kneading a new moon

# The Wood Mountain Series

The Wood Mountain Series honours Andrew Suknaski, and is named after his birthplace in Saskatchewan. Andrew Suknaski has written many fine books, including **Wood Mountain Poems**, a compelling evocation of his home territory and its people. His writing and the two National Film Board films about him have brought him well-deserved national acclaim.

Andy deserves recognition for another kind of work as well — his work in publishing other writers. For many years before there were literary presses on the prairies, Andy edited, typed, designed, printed, stapled and distributed his publications — a "little magazine" called **Elfin Plot** and a series of chapbooks presenting the work of such new poets as Gary Hyland and Glen Sorestad. Through his enthusiasm and generosity, and through the example of his own work, he helped launch many new writers. He did this with no financial support and little recognition.

Coteau Books believes it is important to continue to present these new voices. We began the Wood Mountain Series in 1984 with the publication of **Double Visions**, poetry by Thelma Poirier and Jean Hillabold. This was followed by **What We Bring Home** by Judith Krause, **Standing On Our Own Two Feet** by William B. Robertson, and **Shaking the Dreamland Tree** by Nadine McInnis. We are proud to present the fifth title in the Wood Mountain Series, **The Fire Garden** by Paul Wilson.

The THUNDER CREEK CO-OP is a production co-operative registered with the Saskatchewan Department of Co-operatives and Co-operative Development. It was formed to publish poetry, prose, songs, and plays.

Publications

THE FIRE GARDEN, a moving first book of poetry by Paul Wilson, fifth in the Wood Mountain Series. $7.00 pb. $15.00 hc.

HERSTORY 1988, a practical and informative calendar featuring women in Canada. $8.95 coil-bound.

SOME OF EVE'S DAUGHTERS, third in the McCourt Fiction Series, compelling stories by a striking new voice, Connie Gault. $8.95 pb. $16.95 hc.

THE OLD DANCE. Love stories of one kind or another, 30 short stories which examine love, edited by Bonnie Burnard. $4.95 pb.

HEADING OUT. The New Saskatchewan Poets, a sparkling anthology of poetry, edited by Don Kerr and Anne Szumigalski. $9.95 pb. $15.95 hc.

SHAKING THE DREAMLAND TREE, number four in the Wood Mountain Series, a strong first collection of poetry offering evocative images of a harsh reality, by Nadine McInnis. $7.00 pb.

STANDING ON OUR OWN TWO FEET, third in the Wood Mountain Series, poetry of everyday experiences, by William B. Robertson. $7.00 pb. $15.00 hc.

CHANGES OF STATE, powerful, arresting poetry by internationally-acclaimed poet Gary Geddes. $7.00 pb. $15.00 hc.

WHAT WE BRING HOME, the second book in the Wood Mountain Series, well-crafted poetry by Judith Krause. $7.00 pb. $15.00 hc.

VOICES & VISIONS, interviews with Saskatchewan writers, by Doris Hillis. $11.95 pb. $17.95 hc.

QUEEN OF THE HEADACHES, short stories nominated for the 1985 Governor General's Literary Award, by Sharon Butala. $5.95 pb.

MONSTER CHEESE, a fast-paced, illustrated children's story, by Steve Wolfson. For ages 3-8. $5.95 pb. $11.95 hc.

PRAIRIE JUNGLE, an anthology of songs, poetry, and stories for children ages 6-12, edited by Wenda McArthur and Geoffrey Ursell. $7.95 pb.

HOLD THE RAIN IN YOUR HANDS, a definitive collection of the best from five earlier books, plus new poems, by Glen Sorestad. $8.95 pb. $15.95 hc.

TERRITORIES, fresh, distinctive poetry by Elizabeth Allen. $6.00 pb.

DOUBLE VISIONS, the first release in the Wood Mountain Series, poetry by Thelma Poirier and Jean Hillabold. $6.00 pb. $14.00 hc.

KEN MITCHELL COUNTRY, the best of Ken Mitchell. $4.95 pb.

MORE SASKATCHEWAN GOLD, exciting, imaginative, masterful short stories by Saskatchewan writers, edited by Geoffrey Ursell. $4.95 pb.

FOREIGNERS, a lively, passionate novel by Barbara Sapergia. $4.95 pb.

STREET OF DREAMS, poems that recover our lost experiences, our forgotten dreams, by Gary Hyland. $7.00 pb. $15.00 hc.

FISH-HOOKS the second release in the McCourt Fiction Series. thirteen stories by an exciting new talent. Reg Silvester. $6.00 pb. $14.00 hc.

100% CRACKED WHEAT. an excellent source of dietary laughter from Saskatchewan writers. edited by Robert Currie. Gary Hyland. and Jim McLean. $4.95 pb.

THE WEATHER. vibrant. marvellous poems by Lorna Crozier. $6.00 pb.

THE BLUE POOLS OF PARADISE. a document of secrets. poems by Mick Burrs. $6.00 pb.

GOING PLACES. poems that take you on a vacation with Don Kerr. $6.00 pb. $14.00 hc.

GRINGO: POEMS AND JOURNALS FROM LATIN AMERICA. by Dennis Gruending. $6.00 pb.

NIGHT GAMES. the first book in the McCourt Fiction Series. stories by Robert Currie. $7.00 pb.

THE SECRET LIFE OF RAILROADERS. the funniest poems ever to roll down the main line. by Jim McLean. $5.00 pb.

BLACK POWDER: ESTEVAN 1931. a play with music by Rex Deverell and Geoffrey Ursell. $5.00 pb.

EARTH DREAMS. startlingly original poems by Jerry Rush. $5.00 pb.

SINCLAIR ROSS: A READER'S GUIDE. by Ken Mitchell. With two short stories by Sinclair Ross. $7.00 pb.

SUNDOGS. an anthology of the best in Saskatchewan short stories. edited by Robert Kroetsch. $7.95 pb.

SUPERWHEEL. the musical about automobiles. with script by Rex Deverell and music and lyrics by Geoffrey Ursell. $5.00 pb.

NUMBER ONE HARD. an LP of songs by Geoffrey Ursell from the original Globe Theatre production. $6.00.

EYE OF A STRANGER. poems by Garry Raddysh. $4.00 pb.

ODPOEMS &. poems by E.F. Dyck. $4.00 pb.

All the above may be ordered from your favorite bookstore or from:

coteau books

Thunder Creek Publishing Co-operative
Box 239 Sub #1
Moose Jaw Saskatchewan
S6H 5V0

# About the author

Born in 1954. Paul Wilson grew up in Mirror.
Alberta. and studied communications at
Lethbridge Community College. He works as
Program Director for the Saskatchewan Writers
Guild.

His poems have appeared in numerous
periodicals. and were featured in the Coteau
Books anthology of new Saskatchewan poets.
*Heading Out*: they have been broadcast on CBC
radio and won prizes in Saskatchewan Writers
Guild literary competitions. Wilson has received
the Anne Szumigalski and W.O. Mitchell bursaries
to attend the Saskatchewan School of the Arts.
He has also written articles for *Briarpatch* and
*NeWest Review*.

A member of the poetry group *The Correction Line*.
Paul Wilson also plays for the Saskatchewan
Rough Writers volleyball team and is a past
president of the Regina Guild of Folk Arts. He
lives in Regina with Elizabeth George.

Photo by James Clark